I0119315

(State). Legislature New York

Proceedings of the Legislature of the State of New York

(State). Legislature New York

Proceedings of the Legislature of the State of New York

ISBN/EAN: 9783744712217

Printed in Europe, USA, Canada, Australia, Japan

Cover: Foto ©Suzi / pixelio.de

More available books at **www.hansebooks.com**

In Memoriam.

Hamilton Fish.

PROCEEDINGS

OF THE

LEGISLATURE

OF THE

STATE OF NEW YORK

IN MEMORY OF

HON. HAMILTON FISH,

HELD AT THE

CAPITOL, THURSDAY EVENING, APRIL 8, 1894.

ALBANY:
JAMES B. LYON, PRINTER.
1894.

JOINT COMMITTEE OF THE LEGISLATURE.

SENATE COMMITTEE.

CHARLES T. SAXTON,   JOHN LEWIS CHILDS,

HARVEY J. DONALDSON,   AMASA J. PARKER,

JOHN F. AHEARN.

ASSEMBLY COMMITTEE.

DANFORTH E. AINSWORTH,   S. FREDERICK NIXON,

EDWARD H. THOMPSON,   LAMBERT B. KERN,

OTIS H. CUTLER,   ALBERT A. WRAY,

WILLIAM SULZER,   ROBERT P. BUSH,

EDWARD B. LA FETRA.

PROCEEDINGS

OF THE

LEGISLATURE OF THE STATE OF NEW YORK

IN RELATION TO THE DEATH OF

Hon. HAMILTON FISH.

PROCEEDINGS.

Mr. Saxton offered a resolution in the following words:

Whereas, The Legislature has heard with deep regret of the death, on September 7th last, of the Honorable Hamilton Fish, who had filled with great distinction the offices of Governor of this State, Senator in Congress, and Secretary of State in the National Government.

Resolved (if the Assembly concur), That a joint committee of the Legislature, consisting of five Senators and nine Members of Assembly, be appointed by the presiding officers of the respective Houses to arrange a suitable memorial of the deceased statesman and report what further action shall be taken with reference thereto, and further

Resolved (if the Assembly concur), That a cordial invitation be and hereby is extended to the Honorable George F. Edmunds, of Vermont, to deliver an oration upon the life and public services of the deceased at a time and place to be provided by said joint committee.

9

In Memoriam.

The PRESIDENT put the question on the adoption of said resolution and it was unanimously adopted by a rising vote, and ordered sent to the Assembly for their concurrence.

The Assembly subsequently returned the concurrent resolution relative to the death of Hon HAMILTON FISH with a message that they have concurred in the passage of the same.

The PRESIDENT appointed as the committee on the part of the Senate to act with the Assembly to arrange memorial exercises in honor of the late HAMILTON FISH, Messrs. Saxton, Childs, Donaldson, Parker and Ahearn.

Mr. SPEAKER appointed as the committee on the part of the Assembly, Messrs. Ainsworth, Nixon, Thompson, Kern, Cutler, Wray, Sulzer, Bush and La Fetra.

At a meeting of the above joint committee it was decided to hold a memorial service in the Assembly chamber at such time as would suit the convenience of Hon George F Edmunds, of Vermont, who

Hon. Hamilton Fish.

was invited by the committee to deliver
the memorial address.

The Hon. George F. Edmunds accepted
the invitation and named Thursday evening,
April 5th, as the date for the memorial
service.

11

MEMORIAL SERVICE.

The Legislature having met in joint session in the Assembly chamber, in pursuance of the arrangements made by the joint memorial committee, Roswell P. Flower, Governor, and State officers being present, the meeting was called to order by Hon. Charles T. Saxton, chairman of the joint committee.

The hymn, "Lead Kindly Light," was sung by the choir of Saint Peter's church of Albany.

Prayer was offered by Rt. Rev. William Croswell Doane, Bishop of Albany, as follows:

Almighty and everlasting God, we yield unto thee most high praise and hearty thanks for the wonderful grace and virtue declared in all thy saints, who have been the choice vessels of thy grace and the lights of the world in their several generations; most humbly beseeching thee to give us grace so to follow the example of their steadfastness in thy faith, and obedience to thy holy commandments, that at the day of the

In Memoriam.

---

general Resurrection, we, with all those who are of
the mystical body of thy Son, may be set on His
right hand, and hear that His most joyful voice:
Come, ye blessed of my Father, inherit the kingdom
prepared for you from the foundation of the world.
Grant this, O Father, for Jesus Christ's sake, our only
Mediator and Advocate. Amen.

The anthem, "Eia Mater," was rendered
by the choir.

Hon. Charles T. Saxton, in introducing
Hon. George F. Edmunds, of Vermont,
spoke as follows:

Hamilton Fish was a notable figure both
in our State and in our National politics.
He rendered invaluable services to his
country and won enduring fame as a broad-
minded, sagacious and patriotic statesman.
We point with pride to the fact that he
was a citizen of our State, and have taken
this method of testifying to our respect for
his memory. Let us congratulate ourselves
that we have with us this evening a dis-
tinguished gentleman whose long and honorable public career is known to every one
present, and who was for many years the
personal and political friend of our deceased

fellow citizen. I refer to the Honorable George F. Edmunds, of Vermont, one of the best known of living Americans, who is here by invitation of the Legislature. I esteem it an honor to introduce him to this audience and I am sure we all feel it a great privilege to have the opportunity of listening to him on this interesting occasion.

Hon. George F. Edmunds then delivered the following memorial address:

Mr. PRESIDENT AND GENTLEMEN OF THE LEGISLATURE.—To officially commemorate the lives and public services of those citizens of the State who have been deservedly conspicuous in promoting the progress and welfare of its people is a pleasant and useful duty; and the duty and pleasure are still larger when the citizen who is thus brought vividly into remembrance has impressed his intelligent and patriotic thoughts upon the principles, policies, and movements of a nation,— a nation in which and of which the people of the State of New York have been from the Colonial and Revolutionary days, of more

---

than a century ago to the present time, a most important and valuable component part, both in their character as a State sovereign in all the constitutional respects so wisely and carefully allotted by the founders of the Republic, and as citizens of a united and indivisible community with common interests, with common affections, with common hopes, and a common destiny, embracing all the dwellers in a land of States and people extending from the stormy eastern coasts of the continent where landed Pilgrims and Puritans upon New England shores — the Dutch on Manhattan, the Swedes in Delaware, Royalists along the Chesapeake, and Huguenots upon the southern coasts — to the smiling shores of the tranquil sea where the pious missionaries of the Spanish Regime were at the same time extending their conquests of religion, civilization, and peace among the untutored natives of the land.

Such a citizen was Hamilton Fish.

Deeply and gratefully sensible of the great honor you have done me in con-

nection with this occasion, and sincerely
diffident of my ability to be worthy of
it, I shall, in the short time that can be
properly occupied with the subject this
evening, endeavor to set forth something
of the life and character of the man
whose memory we have assembled to commemorate, in connection with important
events which he to a large and often
commanding degree influenced and shaped
to lasting and useful ends.

Mr. Fish was born in the city of New
York on the third day of August, 1808.
His parents were descendants — on one side
English and on the other Dutch — of the
most respectable and influential of the
inhabitants of Southeastern New York.
His father, Colonel Nicholas Fish, was, during the Revolution, a trusted and gallant
lieutenant of Washington and the intimate
friend and companion of Hamilton, for
whom Mr. Fish was named. His mother
was a lineal descendant of Petrus Stuy-
vesant, the last Governor of New York
under the colonial rule of the Dutch,—an

---

example of that social union and unity of different nationalities that happily followed the termination of the contests for supremacy at the great maritime gateway of the country, the prosperity and happiness of which very largely depended upon the peaceful unity of effort both in social and public affairs among all its people.

Mr. Fish received his instruction preparatory for college at the famous school of Monsieur Bancel, an exiled French Legitimist, and thus acquired in his boyhood that well-grounded and lasting knowledge of the French language that became so useful to him in his administration of the Department of State fifty years later. After due preparation he entered Columbia College, and was graduated in 1827 with the highest honors. He immediately commenced the study of law in the office of Peter A. Jay. the eldest son of the Chief Justice, and was called to the bar of New York three years later. He formed a law partnership with William Beach Lawrence, the learned editor and com-

mentator of Wheaton's International Law,
who had been then recently Secretary of
Legation at London while Albert Gallatin
was minister. Mr. Fish devoted himself
chiefly to chancery and real-estate practice,
besides (as we must conclude from his
display of vast and accurate knowledge
of public law when he first came to the
Secretaryship of State) giving much time
to the study of international law which
his association with Mr. Lawrence would
naturally lead him to do.

At that time the country was divided
into two political parties, the Whigs and
the Democrats, and upon issues involving
the protection and development of home
industries and the creation and extension
of internal improvements to the end of
making the commercial intercourse and the
political and social solidarity of the
country more easy and complete. The
railway was in its earliest infancy, and
the telegraph was unknown; and the use
of steam as a means of water transporta-
tion had small development.

In Memoriam.

Mr. Fish belonged to the Whig party, and gave whatever of assistance he could to the promotion of the policies that appertained to it. During the period of those earliest years at the bar the execution of the customs laws had brought on a crisis between the powers of the National Government and those of the States, manifested in the effort of South Carolina to nullify the laws of Congress. These events led Mr. Fish to the study of the structure of the government and the relation of its various parts and functions as partitioned and adjusted between the United States and the several States, in all their aspects, as well foreign as internal. Thus in the earliest years of his professional career he laid the foundation for that steady growth in the knowledge of the principles and application of constitutional and public law which made him when he came to the great responsibilities of important public station the master of the numerous questions — often unique and difficult — which so continually arose.

Hon. Hamilton Fish.

In 1834, at the age of twenty-six, he was the Whig candidate for the Assembly from a district of his native city, but was beaten.

On the 15th of December, 1836, Mr. Fish was married to Miss Julia Kean, daughter of Mr. Peter Kean, of Ursino, near Elizabethtown. N. J., whose father, John Kean, as a member from South Carolina of the Continental Congress. was one of the committee which reported the famous ordinance of 1787, prohibiting slavery in the Northwest Territory.

During the years that followed he took his full part in the labors of a good citizen in the promotion of the interests of Columbia College and of the Protestant Episcopal Church, of which he was a member, and in the establishment and progress of public libraries and other public institutions and charities in the then and still greatest city of the country.

The wave of great industrial and financial prosperity in the country which had culminated under President Jackson's administration, and resulted in a distribution of public moneys among the States, fell into the trough of general disaster and bankruptcy in 1837–38, during the administration of Mr. Van Buren, and changed the currents of political action, so that at the age of thirty-four, in 1842, he was elected to Congress from a district in the city of New York. At the next election he was beaten on party lines. In 1846 he was nominated for Lieutenant-Governor of New York by the Whig State Convention, but was defeated, owing to the defection of the anti-renters though his associate on the ticket,—Governor Young was elected. But a year later, in 1847, Lieutenant-Governor Gardiner having resigned, Mr. Fish was elected Lieutenant-Governor, at the age of thirty-nine, by a majority of about thirty thousand. In 1848 he was selected by the Whigs as candidate for Governor, and ran against such worthy competitors as John A. Dix, the Free-Soil candidate, and Reuben H. Walworth, Democrat. He was elected, and at the age of forty-one began his duties in that very important and responsible position on the first of January, 1849. At that time, following the election of Taylor and Fillmore, the stress of the slavery question, particularly in respect of the extension of slavery into territory where it did not previously exist, had become great, and the increasing aggressiveness of the slave-holding States and their people in respect of extending the geographical area and the political power belonging to that institution had become so open and manifest that the people of the free States became aroused to a larger comprehension of the incompatibility — indeed impossibility — of carrying on a peaceful and homogeneous National Government under circumstances of social and political institutions so utterly adverse and irreconcilable. It gradually came to be understood by the intelligent people of the country that these differences of situation and of tendency were inherent in the two systems, and that what Mr. Seward

---

later described and characterized as an irrepressible conflict could never be ended, or indeed even stayed, if the further expansion of slavery into free territory should take place. Governor Fish was deeply sensible of the perils of the situation, as he was, also, strongly impressed with the constitutional rights and duties, of whatever kind in respect of the institution of slavery, that the original compact had set forth in the constitution of the common country. To illustrate this I will read some extracts from his messages to the Legislature while Governor.

He says, "The compromises of the Constitution, as they are familiarly termed, do not of right extend to territory beyond the limit of the original thirteen States. The privileges which they concede may be granted, but can not be claimed for any newly-acquired territory."

Again, " If there be any one subject upon which the people of the State of New York approach near to unanimity of sentiment, it is in their fixed determination to resist the extension of slavery over territory now free. With them it involves a great moral principle, and overrides all questions of temporary political expediency. None venture to dissent, and in the mere difference of degree in which the sentiment receives utterance it has proved powerful even to the breaking down of the strong barrier of party organization."

And again, "They are now asked to become parties to the extension of slavery over territory already free. Their answer may be read in their past history. I believe that it is almost, if not entirely, the unanimous decision of the people of this State that under no circumstances will their assent be given to any action whereby the institution of slavery shall be introduced into the territory of the United States from which it is now excluded.

"It is no new declaration in behalf of the State of New York that she regards slavery as a moral, social, and political evil. * * * Regarding it as a domestic relation, founded and limited to the original terri-

torial lines of the State,—dependent for
its continuance and its regulation upon
the legislation of the several States,—New
York exercised her exclusive power over
the institution within her own borders, but
has carefully avoided interfering with the
right of any other States to regulate their
policy in their own way,—not because her
repugnance to human bondage or her attachment to the principles of universal freedom
were confined to the limits of her own
jurisdiction, but because of her attachment
to the union of the States, and because
of her strong regard for the compact into
which she had entered with those States."

He declares that "by the treaty with
Mexico the Territories of New Mexico and
California came to us free; and the laws
of Mexico abolishing slavery, which were
in force at the time of the cession, continue to be operative and are not affected
by any transfer of sovereignty over the
Territory."

He refers to the resolutions of the Legislature of the State in the same direction,

and says, "New York loves the union of the States. She will not contemplate the possibility of its dissolution; and sees no reason to calculate the enormity of such a calamity. She also loves the cause of human freedom, and sees no reason to abstain from an avowal of her attachment While, therefore, she holds fast to the one, she will not forsake the other."

These were great and noble expressions, and, coming from the chief magistrate of the most powerful and populous State of the Union, could not have failed to exert immense influence in favor of constitutional liberty. They illuminate and illustrate the character of the man as a constitutional lawyer, as a patriotic statesman, and as a lover of justice and humanity for their own sakes.

His term as Governor expired on the 1st of January, 1851, and without solicitation or effort on his part he was nominated by the Whig members of the New York Legislature for the office of Senator for the term commencing on the 4th of March of

that year. The state of parties at that
time was peculiar. The great struggle in
respect of the extension of slavery had
reached the stage where President Fillmore
had signed the so-called compromise
measures of 1850; and the important consideration remained as to how far the judgment of the people and the action of Senators
and Members in Congress would support
that measure to the end of its being, as
its friends fondly but illusively hoped it
would be, a final settlement of the trouble.

President Fillmore had, on the occasion
of his signing the measure in the September
preceding, in reply to a letter of congratula-
tion from Mr. Fish on the termination of
the struggle, written to him explaining his
views and motives in respect of signing the
bill, and stating his belief that it would
restore harmony and peace to the country.

Upon the nomination of Mr. Fish for
Senator it was found, when the matter came
to a vote in the two Houses of the Legislature, that while he had a large majority
in the Assembly, he lacked one of such

majority in the Senate, which was so closely divided between parties that the defection of a single Whig left the Senate a tie. This defection occurred, and the Lieutenant-Governor, being a Democrat, concurring with his own party, left the matter in the condition where no joint Assembly could be had, as at that time there was no Act of Congress, as there is now, providing for such a state of things.

The one Whig who, we must presume, thought himself unable to vote for Mr. Fish was concerned as to what the attitude of Mr. Fish would be in respect of standing by these compromise measures as a final settlement of the controversy; and, of course, that attitude would be largely important to the Democratic members of the Legislature, some of whom were what was called Free-Soilers, and others of whom were in strong sympathy with the views and wishes of the slave-holding States. Mr. Fish had been a great admirer of Mr. Clay, whose course had been so largely instrumental in the passage of the so-called compromise measures;

and the Whig Senator who had declined to vote for Mr. Fish was understood to be largely under the influence of Mr. Clay's wishes and opinions. Mr. Clay went so far as to write a private letter to the Collector of the Port of New York, certainly strongly encouraging, if not advising, that this Senator should require as the sole condition on which he would vote for Mr. Fish that Mr. Fish's views and intentions should be publicly stated. This letter was used adversely to Mr. Fish, and came to his knowledge. Mr. Fish then wrote a calm and vigorous letter to Mr. Clay in respect of that kind of interference, and said " I have desired no concealment of my opinions upon the various important measures of the last session of Congress, nor (although Mr. * * * *, his employes, and certain other disappointed aspirants for the Senatorship may affect ignorance, or may assert that my views have been withheld) has there been any concealment. It is true that since the adoption of those measures I have had no occasion for a public or official expression of opinion. It is neither in accordance with my habits nor my taste to protrude myself or my opinions upon the public, but I have both in conversation and in correspondence expressed my opinions very freely both upon the propriety, policy and details of several measures of the last Congress, and upon the imperative and absolute importance of the enforcement of all laws, however distasteful they may be to sectional feelings, and of the strictest regard for the supremacy of the law. * * * While the election was immediately pending I certainly did decline to be interrogated. * * * While a candidate I declined answering any. I had not offered or been instrumental in making myself a candidate for the United States Senate. I had asked no gentleman to vote for me. I held a position entirely too elevated and dignified to be the object of even securing personal interference or solicitation on the part of the candidate. Because I had no public opportunity of expressing any opinions on those questions, I would not do so on the eve of the election, lest the expression might be supposed to be directed so as to influence those who were to vote upon the question. I therefore prefer to refer all inquirers to what I had previously said and written, and to let them judge me by my past action in life and by the opinions I had officially expressed upon all questions upon which it had become necessary to express opinions while I have been in any public position. * * * * The State may be left with but one Senator, or, possibly, a Free-Soil Democratic Legislature may next year send one of their faith; but high as I esteem a seat in the United States Senate, I hold my own honor and character too high to attain that seat by what I should deem a sacrifice of consistency or of self-respect."

This brave and independent attitude of Mr. Fish continued without variation or shadow of turning until after the middle of March, 1851, when he was elected.

During his six years in the Senate Mr. Fish labored quietly and faithfully in the service of his country, and did it in many ways which time does not permit me to enlarge upon. More service, perhaps, than many others who spoke more and labored less.

Prince Bismarck is reported to have said at Versailles, in 1871, that "the gift of eloquence has done a great deal of mischief in parliamentary life. Everything that is really to be done is settled beforehand in the committees, and the speeches in the House are delivered for the public in order to show what the speaker is capable of, and still more for the newspapers in the hope that they may praise. Is the poet or improvisatore exactly the sort of person to whom the helm of State, which requires cool, considerate manipulation, should be confided?"

It was during this period that the Whig party, as a distinct organization, ceased to exist. The unavoidable growth and development of the great conflicts of moral and political affairs that the institution of slavery necessarily created had reached a magnitude that entirely overshadowed all

those questions that in earlier and quieter
times had divided opinions, although in
respect of such questions the principles and
declarations of the old Whig party had all
the time continued to be the same. Hold-
ing to those principles and declarations,
Mr. Fish was reluctant to give up that
organization, and believed that in time,
and with it, upon the principles stated in
his messages as Governor to which I have
adverted, the peace and unity of the nation
could be preserved and its material interests
advanced; but as the ultimate designs of
the slave-holding propagandists grew more
and more manifest, he cheerfully came into
the Republican organization in 1855-56,
and gave all the strength of his great
influence in aid of the effort to elect the
Republican candidate for president, General
Fremont.

His change, or rather transfer, of position
had not been rapid, but it was in keeping
with and illustrative of what has been shown
in his whole career,—that he rarely, if
ever, had occasion to retrace his steps.

Hon. Hamilton Fish.

At the expiration of his term as Senator, on the 4th of March, 1857, he with his family visited Europe, and increased his already large knowledge of foreign countries and foreign affairs by personal observation and intercourse. He returned in time to give his earnest and effective aid to the election of President Lincoln.

When the Rebellion broke out in the spring of 1861, desiring no office, and ambitious of no perferment, he united in the formation in the city of New York of the Union Defense Committee, and soon afterwards, when General Dix, its first chairman, went into the military service, he became the chairman of the committee. This committee in its influence and labors was of immense value to the Union cause, for it, in a large degree, filled the interval between the sudden commencement of war, when the national authorities were unprovided with means and appliances for its vigorous prosecution, until systematic government arrangements and operations could be undertaken and carried on. It might

almost be said that it was of more value
than any one army in the field, for it
arranged and provided for the raising and
forwarding of troops, and attended to the
thousand indispensable incidents and neces-
sities attendant thereon. In this work
Mr. Fish was constant and devoted.

Later in the war of the Rebellion,
Mr. Fish was the leading member of the
commission appointed by President Lincoln
to arrange with the Rebel authorities for
the exchange of prisoners. There had been
great difficulty in respect of this matter
on account of the circumstance that at
least some of the heads of the executive
departments of our government were under
the impression that an arrangement for the
exchange of prisoners would be a measure
which of itself would amount to an acknowledgment of a state of public war, and
would, therefore, embarrass the United
States in the attitude that they occupied
in respect of the action of foreign powers.
But as we can now see it, it is plain to
everybody that after the first few months

of hostilities there was a state of war which, by whatever name it might be called, and however it might affect the relations and duties of foreign powers, every sentiment of humanity must consider not only to warrant but to demand an arrangement between the conflicting powers for the exchange of their respective prisoners. It was to endeavor to effectuate such ends that Mr. Fish and his associate commissioners were sent to confer with the Confederate authorities. Through his efforts and those of his associates an arrangement for the exchange of prisoners was agreed upon, which continued from that time to the close of the war.

We now come in historical order to the career of Mr. Fish as Secretary of State, covering, except six days, the whole of General Grant's terms as President from the 4th of March, 1869, to the 4th of March, 1877.

When Mr. Fish was asked to take the office of Secretary of State, he had not had the slightest wish or expectation of being called upon for that service, and his correspondence with the President on the subject shows with how great reluctance he accepted the office, as well as for what a short period of time he expected to perform its duties. At first he declined it, but General Grant immediately and urgently repeated his invitation, and before Mr. Fish had had an opportunity to again decline, sent his name to the Senate for confirmation, which immediately took place. In view of the embarrassments which had already occurred in respect of the place and of that of the Secretary of the Treasury, Mr. Fish consented to undertake, for a short time, the duties of the most important of the departments of the government, reserving the permission held out by the letter of the President that he could "withdraw after the adjournment of Congress." He continued, however, to serve his country through the whole period I have named, and, with one exception, was the only head of a department who continued to do so. This continued service did not arise from any wish of his, or through any change in his desire to return to private life. The correspondence and papers upon the subject, which I have had the opportunity to peruse, as well as my own personal knowledge, enable me to say that repeatedly, from time to time, and from year to year, Mr. Fish asked the President to consent to his withdrawing from the heavy cares, responsibilities and embarrassments of the station; and once or twice it went so far that the President had consented to his withdrawal, and had looked for a successor: but finding that no safe and satisfactory arrangement could, as the President thought, be made for a new incumbent, he appealed to Mr. Fish to withdraw his resignation and continue to give him the benefit of his service: and once, even this appeal it was thought wise to reinforce by the urgent and concerted entreaties of many of the friends of the President and of Mr. Fish in the Senate

When President Grant came into office there were pending, aside from the great

and difficult questions of reconstruction, two
questions of foreign relations of very large
moment. One was the matter with Great
Britain in respect of the conduct of that
government during the war of the Rebellion,
by its having, after a hasty acknowledgment
of a state of belligerency, permitted the
fitting out of rebel cruisers in its ports,
which cruisers had made indiscriminate
havoc among the unarmed merchant vessels
of the United States. President Johnson
had negotiated a convention with Great
Britain (known as the Johnson-Clarendon
Convention) providing in a certain way for
the settlement of all claims between the
two countries, including those I have
referred to. This convention was pending
in the Senate unacted upon at the accession
of General Grant. It was rejected by the
Senate on the 13th of April, 1869, by (with
the exception of one vote) the unanimous
action of the Senate. Both political parties
concurred in the opinion that it was
entirely inadequate to the occasion, both
in respect of the principles, or perhaps

rather the want of principle, upon which it proceeded, as well as in respect of the confusion and inefficacy of the methods provided for the settlement of the matters involved. The rejection of the treaty led, naturally, to a state of strain and irritability between the two countries that did not augur well for that cordiality and freedom of intercourse that would best promote the welfare of both. It had been contended by some very eminent and influential persons in this country that Great Britain was pecuniarily responsible, beyond her liability for the action of the rebel cruisers, for national losses arising, as it was maintained, from the mere act of her recognizing the Confederacy as belligerents. This was a proposition to which Her Majesty's government would in no manner assent; and now, at this period of time, when the heats of that occasion are subsided, it is obvious that such a doctrine is not one which the United States would find to comport with either their dignity or their interest to adopt. Mr. Fish, while he felt, and stated strongly in his correspondence of the time, the grievous moral wrong of Great Britain in the premature and hasty recognition of belligerency and the consequent enormous injury to the United States occasioned thereby, nevertheless stated privately to his friends the true doctrine upon the subject as follows:

"Public law recognizes the right of a sovereign power, when a civil conflict has broken out in another country, to determine when that conflict has attained sufficient complexity, magnitude and completeness to require (not merely excuse), for the protection of its own interests and peace, and all the interests, relations and duties of its own citizens or subjects, a definition of its relations and of the relations of its citizens or subjects to those of the parties to the conflict. In the exercise of this right the foreign power is responsible to the general obligations of right, and must be guided by facts and not by prejudices," etc.

In this state of unpleasant feeling it required the utmost delicacy and skill of diplomatic treatment to reopen the questions and bring the matter to such a settlement between the two nations as should, upon the principles of public law, be just to the United States.

In May, 1869, Mr. Fish informed Mr. Motley, who had succeeded Mr. Reverdy Johnson as Minister to England, that he thought the question had "reached a point where the important interests of the two countries required some intermission of discussion to allow the excitement and irritation between them to subside."

The situation in this country was rendered specially unpleasant and embarrassing by reason of unfortunate differences and misunderstandings that arose between the President and Senator Sumner, and into which Mr. Fish was unavoidably more or less drawn. This is not the proper occasion for discussing that controversy, even if at any time its discussion would now be useful, but I can say, both from considerable personal knowledge at the time and from a recent perusal of the

private diaries of Mr. Fish, that throughout
it all he endeavored to the utmost of his
power to keep the relations between these
great men pleasant, and to restore them
when they had become strained, and that it
gave him great pain that he was unable to
accomplish his friendly and patriotic purpose.

The interval of repose, as it publicly
appeared, which Mr. Fish thought so desirable after the rejection of the Johnson-
Clarendon treaty, continued until late in
1870, though in the meantime occasional
private correspondence and diplomatic hints
and references to the subject had occurred.
Mr. Motley had been informed that it was
desirable that any further negotiations
upon the subject should be held in Washington rather than in London, and there
had been considerable confidential communication of an entirely unofficial character
upon the subject between Mr. Fish and a
very eminent subject of Her Majesty,
Sir John Rose, and who, doubtless, was
really acting under the authority of the
British foreign office.

Hon. Hamilton Fish.

About the 1st of July, 1870, Mr. Motley was recalled by direction of the President, and General Schenck was appointed to succeed him. The course of affairs during the long interval between the rejection of the Johnson-Clarendon treaty down to the public reopening of negotiations is clearly and concisely stated by Mr. Fish himself in a private letter of the 30th of May, 1871, to Dr. Lieber, as follows: "You have asked me whether the transfer of the negotiations in the Alabama question from London to Washington originated with me. The idea and determination were mine even before the rejection of the Johnson-Clarendon treaty. Soon after I entered upon the office of Secretary of State I saw that that treaty was foredoomed to be rejected. I then decided, and expressed to the President the opinion, that we must take pause in the discussion with Great Britain, and when the excitement and agitation had subsided (which would ensue on the rejection of the treaty), we should insist that any negotiations be held here. In my instructions to

---

Mr. Motley of the 15th of May, 1869, I instructed him to suggest a suspense of the question. On the 28th of June, 1869, I instructed him that when the negotiations should be renewed we desired them to be conducted in this country. * * * * The sending a special mission — some person of high official rank—was suggested by me in May, 1869, and was the subject of close confidential conversation and correspondence with influential persons in England as early as the 1st of June, 1869. The correspondence was continued in this mode until the fruit ripened. The official letters between Sir Edward Thornton and me (which of course were written, received, exchanged, and had passed through the cable word for word before they were sent) finally took date and signature in the latter part of January last. These four letters were the official particulars of twenty months' secret diplomacy."

The correspondence and memoranda covering this period of time, and including the final negotiation of the treaty providing for the settlement of the questions, show that the scheme and form of the treaty were the idea and the work of Mr. Fish, aided, of course, from time to time, by the advice of such gentlemen in public and private life as he thought it fit to consult, and by the very valuable assistance of Mr. J. C. Bancroft Davis, his assistant secretary. In doing this work Mr. Fish had to contend with some most astonishing and extravagant propositions, insisted upon by some gentlemen high in public life as a sine qua non of entering into any negotiations at all. Some of them were such that there is good reason to believe that the mere statement of them to the British government would have put an end to all negotiations at once. And, on the other hand, Mr. Fish had to contend with the astute and earnest efforts of the British government to so frame the treaty as to reduce our chances of success to a minimum. At last, after many consultations and the overcoming of many difficulties, the basis for the appointment of

the Joint High Commission for the purpose
of discussing the mode of settlement and
the adjustment of the differences between
the two countries was completed; and on
the 9th of February, 1871, President Grant
sent to the Senate a statement of the fact,
and his nomination of commissioners on
the part of the United States, of which
commission Mr. Fish was chairman. As
is known, the commission met, and its
efforts in inducing Great Britain to express
its regret for what happened, and in
framing a treaty for the submission of
these subjects of dispute to an international
tribunal were successful. The treaty having
been made, the next step was the framing of the American case. This very
important work Mr. Fish intrusted to his
assistant, Mr. Davis, who performed it,
under the general direction of Mr. Fish,
in the best possible manner. No stronger
statement of the position and rights of
the United States could, I think, have
been set forth by any one. The great
tribunal met at Geneva, and proceeded

with its business. The settlement was at
one time very nearly wrecked by the
refusal of the British government to proceed unless the United States would agree
to withdraw from the consideration of the
tribunal everything connected with indirect
losses, but through the wise and delicate
management of Mr. Fish here, and Mr.
Davis and the American counsel at Geneva
(chief among whom was an eminent New
Yorker, still living, Mr. Evarts), the difficulty was overcome, and a final result
reached by the tribunal honorable to both
countries, and having strong guarantees of
peace among nations by the declaration
of some important principles of public law.
In all this long period of difficulty and
struggle, both within and without the
country, the patience and skill, the fertility
of resource, and the persistent energy of
Mr. Fish were almost marvelous.

During the same time another most
important and embarrassing question —
namely, that of our relations with Spain
in respect of the so-called Cuban revolu-

---

tion — was pressing upon the administration of General Grant and exciting both Houses of Congress. Time does not permit me to go into the subject in any detail. It is sufficient to say that the continuance of peace between the two countries was most seriously menaced. Speeches were made in Congress advocating acknowledging a state of belligerency, and, I believe, advocating the recognition of the independence of Cuba. The Cabinet was divided in respect of the course that should be pursued, and at one time matters had gone so far that a Presidential proclamation was prepared and signed acknowledging a state of belligerency between Spain and Cuba, although at that time the Cuban insurrectionists had neither port, seat of government, nor civil courts, and although belligerency would have given Spain, under the treaty of 1795, rights of search, etc., most injurious to our commerce. Great pressure was brought to bear upon the President to issue such proclamation, and it was current knowledge of the time that

Cuban bonds payable when Cuba should have achieved its independence were finding some kind of a market in the United States with a view of creating interest and influence in support of the scheme. Fortunately President Grant had time for reflection, and upon the earnest and urgent advice of Mr. Fish, instead of issuing the proclamation recognizing the belligerency, he sent a message to Congress stating the real situation, with his views thereon, and then the bubble burst.

Another very important matter of foreign affairs was also engaging the attention of the Administration and of Congress relating to San Domingo. In November, 1869, a treaty was negotiated with that Republic by Mr. Perry, the United States Minister, for its annexation to the United States. In the negotiation of this treaty, General Babcock, the private secretary (military, I think) of the President, was chiefly employed, and Mr. Fish does not appear to have taken any special part further than to cause to be kept out of it a contemplated provision for the annexation of San Domingo as a State of the Union; and sundry other requirements were suggested by him in regard to getting rid of or keeping free from various grants and suspected jobs then thought to exist in and concerning the island. But I think Mr. Fish was in favor of the acquisition of the island as a territory under the dominion of the United States, with a view to our naval and commercial advantage in that quarter of the globe. The treaty was rejected by the Senate chiefly on the ground, as I believe, that the inhabitants of the island were almost wholly incapable of self-government, and still more incapable of taking part in the government of the United States, that their language, habits and customs were entirely different from those of the people of this country, and that the probable result of annexation would be in the not far future the admission of the island as a State, having an equal voice in the Senate with every other State. Whether in view of our

---

increasing interests in the means of inter-
oceanic communication it would not have
been wise to run the risk of possible State-
hood is a question which now very likely
would be decided in favor of taking the risk.

It is true in fact as well as in philosophy
that "alterations in the sentiments of a
people are not effected in a minute or a
year. Even the recognition of the changed
point of view does not involve an immediate or uniformly timed perception of
wherein the new differs from the old.
Nations no more than individuals have the
power nor are they in the habit of study-
ing their shifting moods and tracing the
logical sequence between the aversions of
yesterday, the polite amenities of to-day
and the foreshadowed alliances of to-
morrow."

In 1873-74 the questions concerning the
currency of the United States became
urgent. A panic had occurred in 1873
which had operated disastrously upon the
industry and business of the country, and
the panacea for it was thought by many

of the most eminent personal and political friends of President Grant to be a still further issue of paper money; and a very large body of the people were of the same mistaken opinion. Accordingly, early in 1874, Congress passed a bill commonly known as the Inflation Bill. Very great pressure was brought upon the President to sign it, and equally vigorous were the efforts and protests of those who thought it ought to be vetoed. The President was in great doubt as to what his duty was. He had frequent interviews with Mr Fish upon the subject, and Mr. Fish gave to him fully and cogently the reasons that it appeared to him should compel the President to withhold his approval of it. There is good reason to believe that all the members of the Cabinet, except Mr. Fish and Mr. Creswell, the Postmaster-General, were in favor of the bill being approved. The urgency of the friends of the bill appeared to have prevailed, and the President set about drawing up a message to accompany his approval of the bill, stating his objections to some of its features and finally his reasons for approving it; but after a day or two Mr. Fish was again sent for, and was told by the President that he had been engaged in writing a message giving the best reasons he could find for approving the bill, but that the more he wrote and the more he thought, he was the more convinced that the bill should not become a law; and he was then writing another message refusing his assent to the bill. On the next day, April 21, in the Cabinet meeting, the President stated the conclusion which he had reached, and read the draft of the veto message. A member of the cabinet, who very warmly wished to have the bill approved, suggested that it was always well to lay important papers aside till the next day for further reflection. The President humorously replied that he would do so, and in the meantime would have it copied for signature. On the next day the veto message was signed and sent to Congress. There is no room to doubt that the position and reasons or

---

Mr. Fish were more influential than those of any other one man in inducing the President to take the course he did on that occasion. The wild notion of having a paper currency not redeemable in coin was thus defeated, and the good effect of the veto was soon made manifest by the passage in the next year of the act providing for a resumption of specie payments and the limitation of the amount of the paper money of the government which should thereafter be outstanding. To this measure Mr. Fish gave his most earnest support. The result of that act was that the paper money of the United States soon came to the par of coin and has so continued since.

In the same year, 1875, very serious questions arose in connection with what was called reconstruction, and especially in respect of the State of Louisiana and in regard to the propriety of the military of the United States being employed, even on the call of the Governor of a State, to in any way interfere with the organization or proceedings of a Legislature, or of

a body of men claiming to be a Legislature,
further than to assist in keeping the peace.
On this question Mr. Fish's views were strong
and decided, and had a great effect in pre-
venting the President from taking a position
which might have become a very unfortunate precedent.

In 1876 the Presidential contest between
Mr. Hayes and Mr. Tilden arose, and in
that critical and dangerous time Mr. Fish
was among the most earnest and yet considerate advocates of the creation of the
Electoral Commission. The result of the
action of that commission was the orderly
succession of President Hayes upon principles
of constitutional law which, though then
much disputed, have since been enacted
into permanent law by the almost unanimous vote of both Houses of Congress.

I can not allude to many other interesting and more or less important administrative events occurring during the eight
years of Mr. Fish's administration of the
State Department. I may perhaps, however,
have time to mention one relating to the

expatriation of naturalized citizens. This question was brought prominently into view during the Franco-German war, when Mr. Fish brought into practice what is now generally conceded to be the true principle, and which has been followed by many treaties upon the subject. He maintained that the naturalized citizen, having obtained the privileges of citizenship, was also as fully bound as a native to perform the duties of citizenship, and that, while all the powers of the government should be exerted in defense of the rights of naturalized citizens as fully as in the case of natives, the duties and obligations of the naturalized citizens were precisely as large and as binding as those of natives; and that when naturalization was sought and obtained only for the purpose of exchanging nationality in order that the naturalized citizen might return to and reside in the land of his nativity discharged from all the obligations of his former duties there, he was not deserving of the protection of the government of his adoption.

Hon. Hamilton Fish.

During the last administration of President Grant, Mr. Fish was engaged in important correspondence with the British government on the subject of the Clayton-Bulwer treaty, in which he maintained — with what, I thought, complete and just reason — that the United States were no longer bound by its provisions, and that our relations with the governments of Central America could be carried on without any embarrassments arising from that treaty. A later Secretary (not your great citizen who succeeded Mr. Fish in office), in his correspondence with the British government, appeared to proceed upon the assumption that that treaty was still binding: but the Senate of the United States, during the administration of President Arthur, considered a treaty negotiated by him with Nicaragua for the building of the Nicaragua canal under the auspices and control of the United States, upon the conviction that that treaty was no longer in force: and the treaty received, if I am rightly informed, the affirmative votes of a

---

great majority of the Senate, lacking only three of a two-thirds majority. These events are, I am sure, of much consequence to the United States, in view of the present condition of affairs in that region.

In the winter of 1876-77, Mr. Fish was earnestly engaged in the negotiation of a treaty with the Republic of Nicaragua, looking to the construction of the Nicaragua canal, and the matter went so far that the draft of a convention for that purpose was made up and nearly perfected, when the negotiations were broken off on account of its having been discovered that there were then outstanding grants by the Republic of Nicaragua which would, as Mr. Fish thought, be quite inconsistent with the provisions of the treaty.

Mr. Fish retired from the State Department on the coming in of President Hayes, he and one other (Mr. Robeson) being the only members of the Cabinet of General Grant who had continued in office from the beginning. This period of his public life was, as you will have seen, crowded with

important events and full of diversified difficulties and struggles which often produced
strained relations between governments, and
excited animosities and discordances among
the public men of the United States: and
they were sometimes attended, I am sorry
to say, with suspicions and rumors of selfish
and corrupt motives on the part of some.
It naturally happened, as has, indeed, happened so often in many administrations in
this country and in others, that Mr. Fish
was sometimes the object of bitter attack
and of personal abuse from persons whose
unworthy objects he had resolutely attempted — and generally successfully — to
defeat. But, I believe, Mr. Fish never
made any public reply to such assaults, but
bore them with the calmness that belonged
to a resolute and self-possessed character,
conscious of its own rectitude and contemp-
tuous of the evil tongues of evil men.

In this rapid and necessarily brief review
of the public life of Mr. Fish I have only
mentioned the public stations held by him,
but this short sketch would be incomplete

did I not say that in the whole time of his manhood life he was connected with and active in numerous institutions of business, education, charity, and religion. Among them it may be mentioned that he was president of the general Society of the Cincinnati for nearly forty years, a trustee of Columbia College for more than fifty years, and chairman of its board of trustees for more than thirty years, a trustee of the Astor Library, one of the presidents of the New York Historical Society, and almost constantly a delegate to the Diocesan and General Conventions of the Protestant Episcopal Church and a member of the committee of that church on the revision of the Prayer-Book.

During his residence in Washington his house was always the seat of a most generous and unostentatious hospitality. It was presided over by Mrs. Fish, that most accomplished and gracious lady,— who went to her rest in 1887,—whose memory will always be dear not only to those who had the honor of knowing her in the ordinary walks of official and social life, but to the humble, the poor, and the sorrowful, to whom her sympathies and assistance were always extended with that Christian gentleness and cordiality that illuminate good deeds in a troubled world.

Returning in 1877 to his old city home in New York, and to his beautiful country place in the highlands of the Hudson filled with memories of the revolutionary events in which his father had part, he continued to interest himself in all that makes for the business and social welfare of society, and of the church to which he was so much attached. He continued, also, to feel interest in all public and especially international transactions, and in April, 1882, he had the opportunity to do important service to his country in the matter of the arrests of naturalized citizens of the United States in Ireland. Notwithstanding the strong statements in the American case at Geneva of the adverse attitude of many influential members of the British Cabinet during the Rebellion, which had

In Memoriam.

brought from one of them, who has ever
since been, perhaps, the most powerful of
British Commoners, an unofficial communication to our Minister at London, endeavor-
ing to explain his position, and with what
amounted to a request that Secretary
Fish should modify the statements in the
American case, which had been prepared
by Mr Davis (which modification was not
made). Mr. Fish's great and just reputa-
tion in England enabled him, at a crisis
between the two governments respecting
these arrests, by a simple private telegram
to Sir John Rose, to relieve the tension
then existing and to greatly expedite, if not
absolutely to produce, the immediate release
of most of the Irish-American prisoners.

As I have now rapidly sketched the
principal parts of his public and business
life, I turn with joy to pay (with. I am
sure, all my brother churchmen, and,
indeed, with all Christian men) the tribute
that is most justly due to him for his
life-long and steadfast interest in and
labors for, the promotion and advancement

of church work in the best and most comprehensive sense of that term. He knew that the fundamental doctrines of the gospel, and the works that those doctrines required of every believer, demanded for their best achievements the same sort of organization and systematic administration that are essential in worldly affairs. So he was an active member of the Protestant Episcopal church; not as a bigot or controversialist, but with a large and kindly sympathy and respect for all other Christian churches that with the same true faith were, by methods and in forms different from those of his own church, working in the field of the common Master. In this life-long work the trained powers of his intellect, his business methods, and his great activity came to the service of the sympathies and aspirations of his soul in all the diverse aspects and attitudes of church work, just as his religious character gave, reciprocally, to his business and public labors the illumination of truth, justice, and honor,

In Memoriam.

I have thus endeavored to recall to your view the chief events and incidents in the course of his long and spotless life. The details and associated circumstances of them are most interesting and valuable. It is to be hoped that in due time the contents of his voluminous correspondence and his copious diaries may be made public.

It is amazing that any one man could have done so much in almost every variety of affairs, and always so well. There seems to have been ever present in his mind unlimited and well-ordered stores of historical and political knowledge, and a complete and accurate knowledge of constitutional and public law ready for use on every occasion. He possessed the rare faculty of quickly co-ordinating and arranging in logical order the circumstances of fact with which he had to deal and applying to them the principles of law and justice which related to them; and he thus reached conclusions that he almost never found cause to change. Surely the intellectual tree that bore such fruits—

---

so many and so good — must have been
of the sturdiest oak, with branches wide
and strong, and its roots must have been
grounded in the deepest and purest soil
of the moral and religious character of
man. His courage was always equal to
his convictions. Neither menace nor
calumny, nor flattery, nor self-interest
could swerve or stop him from walking
in the path on which the truest light fell
for him. Thus the great and varied work
he did was easy for him compared with
other men whose course might be affected
by many idle winds of doctrine, or tempests
of passion, or the quicksands of self-
interest. His personal life and character
were pure and self-contained. His manners
were courteous, calm, self-possessed, and
pleasant, and he rarely gave way to the
sometimes proper open manifestation of
feelings of righteous indignation. Such was
the life and character of this citizen to
whose memory we do honor to-night. It
is true that he had extraordinary and
auspicious surroundings at the beginning

of his career; but it is the aggregate of individual lives that make a local society, a state, and a nation; and it is the character of each separate life that makes up the quality and tone of the mass. The accidents of birth, or fortune, or particular opportunity are quite apart from the constant duty of every citizen to do his best for the good of all. The life and conduct of the humblest as well as the highest is an inseparable and an equal element in the great sum of human affairs.

The last few years of his life (shadowed only by his human sorrow in the death of Mrs. Fish, who had been for more than fifty years the beloved sharer of all his joys and solicitudes) were passed in the serenity of contented old age, and in the society of his devoted children. His intellect remained unclouded, and his interest in all good works both public and private, as well as in the lives of his many personal friends, continued to the end. His peaceful death occurred on the 7th day of September, 1893, at his country home on the shores of your beautiful river, when for him the future opened her gateways of gold to the larger and happier life.

From a personal and somewhat intimate acquaintance with Mr. Fish, from the spring of 1869 to the day of his death, I can say, without disparagement of others, that I have never known any man who, all in all,—on every side of his character and behavior,—came nearer to the perfect type of the American citizen and the Christian man.

Your Excellency and the Legislature do well to give high honors to his memory. But what you now do is not a memorial only. His career and the grateful tributes you bestow in the name of the people whom he served so well, are continual inspirations to better lives, higher purposes, and more earnest efforts in your noble State and in our great Republic, to the end that the common welfare and true progress, private and public justice, and civil and political equality, may increase and prevail more and more, until in our beloved

In Memoriam.

land all our ways shall become ways of pleasantness and all our paths are peace.

The exercises were concluded by hymn "God Bless Our Native Land." (America):

God bless our native land !
Firm may she ever stand,
    Thro' storm and night ;
When the wild tempests rave,
Ruler of winds and wave,
Do thou our country save
    By thy great might.

For her our prayer shall rise
To God, above the skies ;
    On Him we wait ;
Thou who art ever nigh,
Guarding with watchful eye,
To thee aloud we cry,
    God save the State. *Amen.*

After which the Rev. W. W. Battershall, D. D., pronounced the following benediction:

The God of peace, who brought again from the dead our Lord Jesus Christ, the great Shepherd of the sheep, through the blood of the everlasting covenant; Make you perfect in every good work to do his will, working in you that which is well pleasing in his sight; through Jesus Christ, to whom be glory for ever and ever. *Amen.*

Hamilton Fish, Jr.
For President

Extension of remarks

of

Hon. Harold Knutson

of Minnesota

in the

House of Representatives

Thursday, August 8, 1935

Letter from

Hon. Royal C. Johnson

a former Representative from South Dakota

(Not printed at Government expense)

United States
Government Printing Office
Washington : 1935

9530—11755

HAMILTON FISH, JR.
FOR PRESIDENT

Mr. KNUTSON Mr. Speaker, in accordance with the consent given me to extend my remarks, I include a letter from former Congressman Royal C. Johnson, of South Dakota. I was so much impressed by the sincerity, soundness, and logic of the views expressed by former Representative Royal C Johnson in this letter written to a friend of his in my State of Minnesota that I have asked permission to print it in the RECORD.

Mr. Johnson was one of the outstanding Members of the House from 1916 to 1933. He was the Republican Chairman of the Veterans' Relief Committee and a member of the Rules Committee. He left Congress to enter the World War and served with distinction as an officer in the 79th Division and was severely wounded in action. After the war on his return to Congress he became the outstanding veteran leader in the Nation. He voluntarily retired from Congress in 1933 to practice law in order to support a growing family.

Royal Johnson was not only an able Representative, but recognized on the Republican side as one of the best politicians in recent years. The reasons advanced by him in support of HAMILTON FISH are those of an experienced Republican leader from the Middle West who served for 13 years with Representative FISH in Congress and knows his qualifications, fitness, and record and understands his unique appeal to the voters.

The letter is as follows:

WASHINGTON, D. C., *April 17, 1935.*

DEAR PAT: Your letter of the 13th, asking for a résumé of the qualifications of the different individuals whose names have been proposed for the Republican nomination for President, came yesterday. Personally, as you know, I am forever out of politics, but I am interested in seeing the Constitution and our form of American Government preserved, and believe that must be done through the Republican Party.

We know we must have a clean, outstanding, comparatively young man, preferably a veteran, who has a background of Americanism, understands government, could execute the administrative duties of the office of President, understands foreign affairs and who can get the votes.

For that reason I am writing you frankly about the man who I think would make a good President and who, I am firmly convinced. can get more votes in the 1936 fall election than any other individual. I am sure that that man is HAMILTON FISH, Jr., present Member of Congress from New York, and I am writing you frankly concerning him because I think that you ought to take up the battle for him in your State, just as one time, some years ago, you enlisted in the marines. I think, Pat, it is your duty.

9530—11755   (2)

3

The following is a statement of my reasons for the suggestion:

PERSONALITY

1. In my judgment, he possesses the qualifications that would make him a good and perhaps a great President.

2. He is 47 years old, physically fit, has been a great football player and a patriotic combat soldier decorated by his country. He is the type that will attract the younger element and the liberal and independent voters.

3. He is a married man with two young children, and he has lived the sort of life that makes it impossible for him to be personally attacked.

LEGISLATIVE RECORD AND POLITICAL AVAILABILITY

1. He was a liberal in Congress when the Republican Party was headed for reactionary defeat.

2. He is fundamentally right on the American system of government and the Constitution.

3. He has practical political experience of three terms in the New York State Legislature (1912–15), as a Progressive follower of Theodore Roosevelt, and 16 years as a Republican Member of Congress from that State.

4. He can do more to cement the service men than any other individual, because he has a fine combat record; was Chairman of the Commission which gave veterans a reasonable civil-service preference; was chairman of the committee which wrote the preamble to the constitution of the American Legion in St. Louis in May 1919; introduced and secured the passage of the resolution returning the body of the unknown soldier now lying in Arlington Cemetery; is now the oldest veteran in point of service in Congress, and has no animosities among service men, who, as you and I know, are subject to them.

5. He is the only man in the United States, in my judgment, who could bring back the colored voters to the Republican Party, because he served with colored troops (Three Hundred and Sixty-ninth Infantry); handled more compensation cases for colored veterans than anyone in the United States; and defended the colored troops on the floor of the House and in public speeches when attacks were made on their military records.

He already has the endorsement of the leading Republican colored leaders of the United States. He introduced a bill in Congress February 23, 1926, which passed the House on April 28, 1926, proposing a monument to colored soldiers.

6. He has the support of the leading German newspapers of the United States, because he came back from France with charity in his heart for a defeated enemy, and on February 8, 1924, introduced a bill appropriating $10,000,000 for relief of distressed and starving women and children of Germany, which passed the House on March 24, 1924, and was enacted into law.

7. Being one of the men who never had particular racial or religious prejudices, he is friendly with many Jewish people because on May 3, 1922, he introduced a bill creating a national home for the Jewish people in Palestine, which became a law on September 21, 1922.

8. He has been a leader in the fight on communism when others paid no attention to it, and introduced at this session a bill in the House, which later the Democrats purloined from him, providing for an investigation of conditions in Mexico, where communism is attempting to eradicate all belief in religion.

9. He is immensely strong with labor and intimate with labor leaders. He voted with them 16 out of 20 times, definitely refusing to go with them on the occasions when small groups of labor leaders attempted to assume the prerogatives of government.

10. He supported social and humanitarian reforms which everyone now accepts should have been secured by labor long ago.

11. He is strong with the Polish people and is the author of the law which passed Congress promoting our representative in Poland

from a minister to an ambassador, and has recently introduced a bill for the erection of an American Embassy at Warsaw.

12. He introduced and passed through Congress a resolution extending congratulations on the hundredth anniversary of the independence of Greece. The official magazine of the Order of Aheppa has publicly thanked him, has publicly supported him, and he has been officially invited to Greece at the expense of that Government, an invitation which he could not accept.

13. He has the support of a vast group of American Italians. Part of this is due to the fact that many Italians who enlisted or were drafted into the American Army were discharged abroad and remained in Italy until they could not legally return to the United States. Mr. FISH led the fight for the passage of a law which allowed thousands of fathers and mothers of naturalized World War veterans to be admitted to the United States, regardless of the quota; that is, the fathers and mothers of those soldiers who had honorable discharges.

14. He represents a dairy and agricultural district, and is a member of the National Grange and Farm Bureau Federation, and has shown both sympathy and interest in the farmers' problems of the Middle West, and recently reintroduced the McNary-Haugen export-bounty bill, and has urged the passage of the Lemke-Frazier farm-refinancing bill. He insists that the Republican Party present a constructive substitute for the A. A. A. before attempting to abolish it.

15. He is the highest ranking Republican on the House Committee on Foreign Affairs, has consistently fought American intervention in European affairs, the League of Nations, and all foreign entanglements and sanctions, and is particularly qualified to represent American thought in world affairs.

16. He has a consistent record of sticking with his friends, sometimes even to his own disadvantage.

17. He is a skilled and fluent public speaker on both platform and radio and has one of the most pleasing radio voices in the United States. In addition, he is smart enough to write his own speeches.

18. He lives in Franklin Roosevelt's district, has led his ticket overwhelmingly every year he has run, carried his district in 1932 by 17,618 votes, increased his majority 2,000 votes in 1934, and led the Republican candidate for Governor by 16,000 votes. In this connection, let me call your attention to what we know, which is that no one can tell why a man can secure votes. We know he either can or he cannot, and it has been demonstrated that people do vote for FISH. He was one of the few Congressmen to run ahead of President Coolidge in 1924 and of President Hoover in 1928.

19. More than 50 Members and ex-Members of Congress who knew him have already endorsed him, and a voluntary campaign committee has recently been formed.

20. I have seen the voluntary letters he has received, and there has been no voluntary support such as he is receiving since the time of Theodore Roosevelt. This is because the Republicans of this country have been looking for a sound individual of his type who has repeatedly demonstrated great vote appeal. I know him, and I know that he is frank, sometimes distressingly frank, but it is a great asset at the present time, and he will speak out and put some color and fire into the campaign.

21. He has for more than a year urged the liberalization of Republican policies within the confines of the Constitution and the necessity of making a direct appeal to Jeffersonian Democrats in defense of their own principles to join the Republicans in ousting the "new dealers" and preserving American constitutional liberty.

As busy as I am, I intend to work in this campaign, because it appears to be a duty; and I believe you ought to take it up with your friends in your State and make one more real American fight.

Sincerely yours,   (Signed) ROYAL C. JOHNSON.

9530—11755   U. S. GOVERNMENT PRINTING OFFICE: 1935

www.ingramcontent.com/pod-product-compliance
Lightning Source LLC
Chambersburg PA
CBHW021523270326

41930CB00008B/1071
* 9 7 8 3 7 4 4 7 1 2 2 1 7 *